Procrastination

First Steps to Change

Resources for Changing Lives

A Ministry of
The Christian Counseling and
Educational Foundation
Glenside, Pennsylvania

RCL Ministry Booklets
Susan Lutz, Series Editor

Procrastination

First Steps to Change

Walter Henegar

P&R
P U B L I S H I N G
P.O. BOX 817 • PHILLIPSBURG • NEW JERSEY 08865-0817

Printed in the United States of America

Library of Congress Cataloging-in-Publication Data

Henegar, Walter.
Procrastination : first steps to change / Walter Henegar.
p. cm. — (Resources for changing lives)
Includes bibliographical references.
ISBN 0-87552-699-3 (pbk.)
1. Procrastination. I. Title. II. Series.

BF575.P95.H46 2004
155.2'32—dc22

2004049544

I've been procrastinating most of my life. If a task is even remotely unpleasant, my instinctive tendency is to put it off. It's not that I'm lazy; I'm actually very busy. I just wait as long as possible to do the really hard stuff.

Several years ago, God gave me the faith, insight, and power to fight this pattern. I was a seminary student in my twenties with a chronically ill wife and two small children. My story unfolds within those particular circumstances, but I believe that the basic heart dynamics are common to many people.

Because it is relatively acceptable in our culture, procrastination is easy to ignore. In fact, for much of my life, I was even perversely proud of it. But procrastination is a serious, deeply rooted pathology that negatively affects almost every area of life. It is an area where I needed to heed the counsel of Colossians 3:9–10, where Paul urges believers to "put off" the old self and "put on" the new self, "which is being renewed in knowledge after the image of its creator." This put off/put on pattern is at the heart of the Christian life—and it works! My procrastinating desires are still strong and seductive, but by God's goodness and grace, I am changing.

As you read my story, consider your own. Do you procrastinate? Ask God to change you, and trust that he is able to do it. Search the scriptures for truth that searches *you*. Study the patterns of your life, and ask others to help you see your situation more clearly. Keep asking God to change you. If he can change me, he can change you, too.

A Procrastinator's Story

Pressure makes diamonds. That was my personal motto in college, where I first began to recognize my pattern of procrastination. I started most of my papers the night before they were due, and I usually got As. My friends teased me about it, but I defended myself with Parkinson's Law: "Work expands to fill the time available for its completion." Why spend a week on a paper if I could spend a night and get the same result?

The working world only reinforced my pattern. Sitting in front of a computer screen all day offered limitless opportunities for procrastinating: e-mail, internet, pointless little games like Minesweeper. As long as I was busy doing *something*, no one would complain if I pulled off the big jobs at the last possible minute. There were a few close shaves, but I was generally a valued (or overvalued) employee.

When I got married, my uncle, who was officiating, joked about my tendency right in the middle of the ceremony. His sermon was about the necessity of change in marriage. Looking right at me, he said, "One who is a procrastinator, if he gets over it, will put that off as long as he can."

And that's exactly what I did, though married life made it more difficult. My designated crunch times now belonged to my wife as well, and I had to push her away to get last-minute work done. Even worse, I began dragging my feet about some of our shared responsibilities, like creating (and sticking to) a budget, praying together, and washing the dishes. I began to feel ashamed, or perhaps I should say defensive. *I mean, everyone knows I'm a responsible guy. This is just a quirk of my personality, right? Can't she just cut me some slack?*

My wife did cut me some slack, but only as much as her chronically ill body would allow.

Repeated hospital stays and constant bouts with pain forced her to lean heavily on me to take care of her and our two children. If marriage is God's chisel for sanctifying us, then children sharpen the edge. The three of them pushed my work responsibilities deeper into my free time and later into the night. I slept less and less. I still managed to pull most things off, but the quality of my work suffered and my list of undone chores grew. I was weary, discouraged, and full of self-pity. A couple of times, I even experienced something like panic attacks. I envied my more disciplined friends but saw little hope of becoming like them.

Then, during my first year in seminary, a counseling class challenged me to give Scripture a shot at diagnosing—and solving—my problem. What captured my imagination was the biblical metaphor of a tree, and the suggestion that my prickly branches of procrastination were being nourished by unseen roots, growing deep in the chambers of my heart. A hope even flashed that I might uncover *the* root, and somehow cut it out once and for all. In retrospect, I see that this second hope reflected my procrastinator's heart, always looking for a shortcut or a silver bullet, but still, I was on the right track.

Initial Insights

To get down to the roots I had to start with the branches. As I studied my life, I gained two unexpected insights. The first was that my procrastinating patterns were highly systematic. They infected every area of my life, and operated in orderly, predictable ways. My heart had its own dysfunctional flow chart of if-thens: *If it's not due tomorrow, then you've got plenty of time. If it's crunch time, then neglect every other responsibility. If you've just finished a big job, reward yourself*, and so on.

Secondly, I realized that I am largely ignorant of this system most of the time. This was hard to take because I've always considered myself an introspective guy, and my procrastination had been on my radar for some time. But I had always defined it as an *absence:* I wasn't working hard enough—or soon enough, at least. The question that hadn't occurred to me was, If something is *absent*, then what is *present?* Those hours were going somewhere—what exactly was I *doing* with them?

I began paying more attention to the way I spent my time, particularly those hours designated for work. I discovered that I usually did *good* things! I would reorganize my desk, return letters, balance the checkbook, or practice guitar. Of course, less noble activities were there, too: an hour of TV, scrounging for junk food, shopping on the internet for things I didn't need. But the "good" activities began to explain how I had justified my procrastination as a necessary evil for an overworked guy.

I also began searching Scripture for insights about work. Not surprisingly, I found numerous verses on the necessity of hard work. One passage in particular jumped out at me. Second Thessalonians 3:11 describes a group of *idlers* or *busybodies* who were not pulling their weight in the young church. The word "busybody" intrigued me, so I looked it up in the original Greek. It's a compound of the verb meaning "to work" and a preposition meaning "around." So the second part of verse 11 could be translated literally, "Such people do no work at all; instead, they *work around*."

All of a sudden I saw myself clearly. As I buzzed around the room, the one thing I needed to do most sat unheeded in the middle of it. I wasn't just a procrastinator; I was a work-around-er.

I remembered reading Charles Hummel's little booklet *Tyranny of the Urgent*. Hummel marveled that Jesus could say on the cross,

"It is finished," even though so much of his kingdom-building work was yet incomplete. Hummel argued that Jesus could say this only because he had done "all the work the Father gave him to do." The connection to my own sin was clear: Unless I'm doing what *God* has called me to do, I'm doing someone else's work. When I procrastinate, I'm *meddling* in things that are "none of my business"—like a busybody.

Digging Deeper

I began to feel like I was really figuring myself out. I'd notice when I started slipping into procrastination, and it was easy enough to stop—at first. But when midterms hit, I found myself pulling all-nighters again, and I was back to square one. Ironically, though, I still had to work on my procrastination for my counseling class. Reluctantly, I dove back in, this time trying to get at the deeper "root" issues.

It wasn't hard to begin naming things. Pride was surely operating; every time I pulled an all-nighter to finish a job, I was protecting my reputation before my friends and superiors. Fear of others was there too. When I had those mild panic attacks, the fear of others' disapproval was foremost in my head. Laziness wasn't the main thing, but it definitely played a part; sometimes I just didn't want to do anything. Pleasure-seeking and Escapism were big players, as well, though I generally confined myself to "acceptable" thrills like watching movies and bingeing on Ben & Jerry's ice cream.

Identifying these heart issues didn't produce the catharsis I had hoped for. Not only were they intimidating (*How could I ever put a dent in pride?*), but they were *internal*, and I still suspected that external factors played a key role. Sometimes I really did have unreasonable amounts of work to do. Even when I planned my time responsibly, unexpected events would often force me to work at the last minute. Sometimes this last-minute work was actually pretty good, and when I started other jobs early, they *did* expand to fill the time.

Taking a different tack, I composed a long list of "if onlys"—circumstances that would make everything better if only they changed. My wife's illness was at the top of the list, followed by the financial constraints of being in graduate school, far from family. This was followed by my unsettled vocational future.

The list kept growing. *As soon as our daughter sleeps through the night, or finishes teething, or gets out of diapers—then I'll have time to start exercising again. When we stop traveling so often and get into a routine, then I'll be able to begin my days in prayer. I'd be a much more disciplined guy, if I only had a mentor to show me how.*

Then the really sinister ones started to emerge. *If my wife were more disciplined, I'd have less to do around the house. If my friends cared enough to ask me about this stuff, I wouldn't struggle so much. If my parents had modeled better work habits, I'd be light-years ahead by now.*

Finally, I uncovered a similar list of excuses that characterized the way I work. *I just need to get this out of my system, and then I'll buckle down. This semester is already a wash, so I'll work on that next semester when I've got a clean slate. The first of the month should be a good time to start that. I'll just set my alarm and do it in the morning.*

Ugh! Those broad categories like Pride and Escapism were taking on specific contours. It wasn't pretty. I started seeing my foolishness, rationalizing, and self-deception everywhere. I began to despair, though I still clung to the hope that things might get better. I just had to get my head on straight.

Theological Truths

My head did need straightening, but now it was theological. God used the words of my professors, the writings of others, and the preaching of my pastor to confront me with my lack of confidence in some essential truths of the Christian faith.

The most significant was my tendency to doubt that God could change me at all. This was an expression of my pride. I didn't really doubt my salvation; I just doubted that much change was possible this side of heaven. If there was an "old self" and a "new self" inside me, the old self clearly had the advantage (see Col. 3:9–10).

But that simply was not true. I was reminded that the New Testament repeatedly characterizes salvation as a decisive shift from death to life, from slavery to sonship (1 John 3:14; Rom. 6:6). While the "tree" of my life will always grow some thorns, I am now fundamentally a *fruit* tree. In Christ I have been genetically re-engineered to produce the fruits of the Spirit, and self-control is one of them (Gal. 5:22)!

Lest I then expect an instantaneous transformation, I was also reminded that Scripture describes sanctification as a *progressive* reality. I always *said* I believed this—"nobody's perfect" is a self-evident truth in any culture—but in practice, I still *expected* to be more sanctified right away. My continual longing for a silver bullet to slay my sin exposed the impatience and laziness of my unbelief in progressive sanctification.

As I recognized my unbelief in these areas, the question now became, "What do I do with what I've discovered?" The unmistakable answer of Scripture was, "Repent." I was already learning that repentance was a gracious gift and a joyful essential of the Christian life. But now, instead of just repenting of clearly definable *acts* of sin, I also began repenting of sinful *attitudes* and dispositions in my heart.

There was no shortage of these, particularly as I uncovered new ways that I rationalized and clung to my procrastinating habits. It wasn't pleasant, but I wasn't afraid of facing my sins any more, now that I regularly experienced the true cleansing of taking them to the cross. I was in an accountability group with two seminary friends, and it became a weekly opportunity to confess to each other and repent to God together. Though I often resisted that initial bending of my knees, I would inevitably become reluctant to leave the posture of prayer. I began to really *experience* the forgiveness of God, and it freed me to pursue him more fervently.

I became convinced that repentance is always the first step in the process of change. Without repentance, I was a guilt-driven man relying on my own strength and my own skewed perception of my problems. With it, I was a grace-driven man with God's strength and a more biblical perception of my problems.

As I continued in this process, my repentance took on a more positive, forward-looking character. As I prayed for God's forgiveness, I thought ahead to future situations where I'd be tempted in the same way, and asked for strength to act wisely when they came.

God answered my prayers, and I really started to change. Even my wife noticed. Rather than forcing myself to complete every unfinished task (or coast until the next "clean slate" came around), I forced myself to accept some losses and focus on absolute top priorities. Now, my time in prayer was at the top of that list, followed by time with my family and adequate sleep. Non-negotiable school assignments followed, and though they weren't as good as they could have been, they weren't altogether bad. I still learned a lot that semester.

Ongoing Change

Since then, I have continued to grow in my understanding and resistance to procrastination, particularly as I've recognized its impact on others. While revisiting that 2 Thessalonians passage about busybodies, I discovered an earlier passage that explained *why* Paul treated the matter so seriously: "so that your daily life may win the respect of outsiders, and so that you will not be dependent on anybody" (1 Thess. 4:12). In other words, procrastination cripples my example to non-Christians *and* my love for the church and my family.

Seeing my failures in these areas not only led to more repentance, but gave me a new awareness of the consequences of my sin. I saw how I had been unloading my responsibilities onto my wife and daughters. I began seeing how many opportunities to love and serve others I had missed because of the disorder in my own life. Every time I broke a commitment or fudged a deadline, I saw how poorly I reflected God's character to a world that already distrusts his people. For the first time I heard Jesus' command, "Let your 'Yes' be 'Yes,' and your 'No,' 'No,' " as a direct extension of the Great Commission (Matt. 5:37; 28:18–20).

As my battle with procrastination advances, I'm learning how to subdue my heart. My whole heart is sinful and unreliable—or as Jeremiah 17:9 says, "deceitful above all things."

Recognizing that unreliability has given me a greater appreciation for the way God uses his people in the sanctification process. I am particularly thankful for close friends, who have a standing invitation to show me my sin and to remind me of the gospel. When I've got a lot of work coming due, I ask them to encourage me to work ahead and to challenge me when I get overwhelmed. Knowing how much I need that outside input has given me greater courage to do the same for them, "speaking the truth in love"(Eph. 4:15).

Just as I had been largely ignorant of the workings of my heart, I had also lost sensitivity to the consequences of neglecting and abusing my body. In that first year of tackling procrastination, I began running three times a week with a close friend. Both of us became better stewards of our physical health, and I lost more than thirty pounds. I haven't entirely sworn off Ben & Jerry's, but I eat much healthier now, and my energy level is more consistent. Lately, I've been working to recognize when I'm full, and (of all things!) to stop eating.

Similarly, I now see sleep as a God-given responsibility, and not something I can sacrifice without cost. When I have to do last-minute work (which still happens, I'm afraid), I'll go to bed around 9:00 p.m. and get up at 4:00 a.m. instead of staying up half the night. That's still seven hours of sleep, and I have several quiet hours left for rested and focused work. I always considered myself a "night person," but it turns out that I work more efficiently in the morning. Following a schedule that's closer to my wife's has also improved our day-to-day sense of companionship.

The Road Ahead

I am profoundly grateful for the change God has worked in this area, though there is much more work to do. My procrastinating desires still tug at me (even as I write these words!), and those years of working under pressure have made working ahead unnatural and inefficient. My ideal is to work with last-minute focus and intensity, but well before the deadline. I don't do that very well yet, and Parkinson's Law still plagues my best efforts.

I also need to regularly re-learn many lessons, particularly the theological ones. It is easy to drift out of a repentant mindset when conspicuous sins don't show up every day. That complacency is something to repent of; a reason to ask God to "search me and know my heart" (Ps. 139:23). Just as I once confronted my unbelief that God could change me, I now need to confront my unbelief that he *wants* to change me "more and more" (see 1 Thess. 4:1). I'm still lazy, proud, and prone to escapism, and those desires won't leave me in this life.

Conclusion

In short, I'm working out my salvation "with fear and trembling," yet with hope and confidence that "it is God who works in [me] to will and to act according to his good purpose" (Phil. 2:12–13). Procrastination is not the only area where I need to change. As a full-time pastor, I am called to live a much more outward-directed and other-centered way of life. I want to fear God and desire to please him more than anyone else. I want "to know Christ and the power of his resurrection and the fellowship of sharing in his sufferings" (Phil. 3:10). I want to become more like Jesus, so that others will come to know him, too.

It won't be easy, but I'm confident that God will do it, because he promised he would.

He might take some time, but *he* doesn't procrastinate.

Questions and Challenges

1. Do you doubt that God can change you in this area of your life? Read some passages such as Romans 6:1–7, Ephesians 3:20–21, Colossians 3:1–4, and 2 Corinthians 3:17–18; 5:17. If there is the smallest doubt in your mind, repent of it specifically, right now, and receive God's mercy in Christ (1 John 1:8–9). Now ask him for more faith (Luke 17:5), for wisdom (James 1:5–8), and for the Spirit's power to begin changing you (Col. 1:29).
2. Do you have a biblical understanding of work and rest? Search the scriptures to broaden or deepen your understanding. Some places to start include Genesis 2:15–25, Exodus 20:8–11, Proverbs 6:6–11, Psalm 127:2, Matthew 25:14–30, and 2 Thessalonians 3. Don't stop until you've gained a fuller picture of the life God is calling you to live.
3. Do you understand the particular patterns of your own procrastination? Watch yourself closely for a week. Keep a journal or a log book of how you actually spend your

time. Ask someone who spends a lot of time with you (a sibling, roommate, coworker, spouse, etc.) what they notice about your habits of work, rest, and play. Write down your observations and ask God to give you clearer sight (see Heb. 3:13; 4:12–13; Eph. 3:17–19).

4. *Why* do you procrastinate? Take two or three examples from the recent past and chase down the main motives of your heart (see Luke 6:44–45). What did you want most in that situation? What outcome did you want most to avoid? Whose opinion mattered most to you? When you begin to identify a desire (such as pleasure, escape, or respect), ask yourself: What does this desire of mine imply about God? What false perceptions of him does it betray?
5. What life changes do you need to make in order to grow in this area? Write down one specific step you can take today to move in that direction. Ask God to empower you to do it. Find a friend who's willing to help.

RCL Ministry Booklets

A.D.D.: Wandering Minds and Wired Bodies, by Edward T. Welch

Anger: Escaping the Maze, by David Powlison

Angry at God?: Bring Him Your Doubts and Questions, by Robert D. Jones

Bad Memories: Getting Past Your Past, by Robert D. Jones

Depression: The Way Up When You Are Down, by Edward T. Welch

Domestic Abuse: How to Help, by David Powlison, Paul David Tripp, and Edward T. Welch

Forgiveness: "I Just Can't Forgive Myself!" by Robert D. Jones

God's Love: Better than Unconditional, by David Powlison

Guidance: Have I Missed God's Best? by James C. Petty

Homosexuality: Speaking the Truth in Love, by Edward T. Welch

"Just One More": When Desires Don't Take No for an Answer, by Edward T. Welch

Marriage: Whose Dream? by Paul David Tripp

Motives: "Why Do I Do the Things I Do?" by Edward T. Welch

OCD: Freedom for the Obsessive-Compulsive, by Michael R. Emlet

Pornography: Slaying the Dragon, by David Powlison

Pre-Engagement: 5 Questions to Ask Yourselves, by David Powlison and John Yenchko

Priorities: Mastering Time Management, by James C. Petty

Procrastination: First Steps to Change, by Walter Henegar

Self-Injury: When Pain Feels Good, by Edward T. Welch

Sexual Sin: Combatting the Drifting and Cheating, by Jeffrey S. Black

Stress: Peace amid Pressure, by David Powlison

Suffering: Eternity Makes a Difference, by Paul David Tripp

Suicide: Understanding and Intervening, by Jeffrey S. Black

Teens and Sex: How Should We Teach Them? by Paul David Tripp

Thankfulness: Even When It Hurts, by Susan Lutz

Why Me?: Comfort for the Victimized, by David Powlison

Worry: Pursuing a Better Path to Peace, by David Powlison

Gideon Haigh

My Brother Jaz

MELBOURNE
UNIVERSITY
PRESS

Melbourne University Publishing acknowledge the traditional owners of the unceded land on which we work, learn and live: the Wurundjeri Woi-wurrung peoples of the Kulin nation. We pay respect to elders and acknowledge the importance of Indigenous knowledge.

MELBOURNE UNIVERSITY PRESS
An imprint of Melbourne University Publishing Limited
Level 1, 715 Swanston Street, Carlton, Victoria 3053, Australia
mup-contact@unimelb.edu.au
www.mup.com.au

First published 2024
Reprinted 2025

Cover design by Sandy Cull
Text design and typeset by Megan Ellis
Printed in China by 1010 Printing Asia Limited

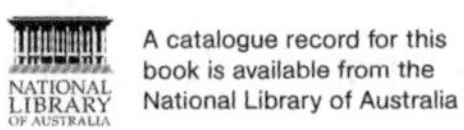

9780522880830 (paperback)
9780522880847 (ebook)